WHAT GOD SAYS™
ABOUT SEX

ERIC ELDER

What God Says™ *About Sex*
Copyright © 2006 Eric Elder.
All rights reserved.

Cover design by Andris Sprogis.

What God Says™ is a registered trademark held by
Eric Elder for a series of inspirational books and audio
recordings. To learn more about this series, visit
WhatGodSays.com

ISBN 978-1-931760-08-9

DEDICATION

To my children who—had I not
learned the things I share in this book—
might never have been born.

Acknowledgments

Special thanks to the following people for their input and encouragement during the creation of this book:

Lana Elder, Bridgette Booth, Larry Booze, Brenda Friend, Brent Knapton, Steve Knight, Al Lowry, Dan Mountney, Linda Olivero, Jessica Pastirik, Russell Pond, Greg Potzer, Sue Roberts, Noah Roberts, Kent Sanders, and Andris Sprogis.

TABLE OF CONTENTS

PREFACE

I began this book as a way to summarize hundreds of letters I've written and conversations I've had regarding what God says about sex. But before I wrote the first word, I asked God who the readers of this book might be. I wanted to be able to picture them in my mind as I wrote these words.

Without hesitation, God spoke to my heart: "Write it for your children."

My children?!? I thought. *That's not who I had in mind at all!*

When I realized that God was serious, my passion and diligence for this project increased a hundredfold. I realized that the readers of this book would not just be people on the far side of the globe who could take or leave these words as they wished. The readers would be my own precious children, the ones I most wanted to see enjoy the fullness of sex without experiencing the pain that has fallen upon so many.

Then God nudged my heart again.

I realized that this would be the same audience *He* wanted to reach through this book: *You, His own precious child, the one He most wants to see enjoy the fullness of sex without experiencing the pain that has fallen upon so many.*

With that in mind, I invite you to read these words that I've written from the depths of my heart.   For they're not only my impassioned words to my beloved children, they're also God's impassioned words to you—His beloved child.

Eric Elder

How to Know What God Says About Anything

*"All Scripture is inspired by God
and is useful to teach us what is true..."*
2 Timothy 3:16a, NLT

I was working on a project a few years ago called *What God Says About Angels.* One day, someone asked me, "How do you *know* what God says about angels?"

It was a great question. How *did* I know what God says about angels? How did I know what God says about *anything?*

For me, whenever I'm ever looking for "a word from God," the first place I look is in the Bible—it has over 800,000 of them! The words in the Bible have given me encouragement and guidance, hope and inspiration, insight and understanding. The Bible has given me more practical wisdom than any other book in the world.

I think this is true for two reasons:

1) *The words of the Bible have stood the test of time.*
   These words were written by people who
   have been extremely close to God—people
   who have asked God honest questions and
   listened for His honest answers. What happened in their lives as a result of hearing
   and doing what God said was phenomenal.
   So phenomenal, in fact, that even to this
   day, thousands of years later, the Bible is
   still the most widely read, published and
   translated book in the world.

2) *The words of the Bible have stood the test of trial
   and error.* My own trial and error! Whenever I've read something in the Bible and have
   wondered if it might work in my own life,
   I've put it to the test. What's happened to
   me as a result of hearing and doing what
   God said has been phenomenal, too, as
   you'll see in this book.

After putting into practice hundreds of things
that I've read in the Bible, I've come to the same
conclusion as the Apostle Paul who wrote:

9

"All Scripture is inspired by God and is useful to teach us what is true and to make us realize what is wrong in our lives. It straightens us out and teaches us to do what is right" (2 Timothy 3:16, NLT).

In perhaps no other area of my life has this proven more true than in the area of what God says about sex.

I'd like to say a special word to those of you who may be learning about sex for the very first time. I've written a special chapter just for you at the end of this book called, "What is Sex, Anyway?" *You'll want to read this special chapter first* as it will give you a good foundation as you go through the rest of this book.

For those of you who already know about sex, you might still want to read this special chapter first. This may be the first time that you've ever heard sex described *like this* and it will give you a good foundation as you go through the rest of your *life*.

1

Why God
Created Sex

*"Delight yourself in the LORD and
he will give you the desires of your heart."*
Psalm 37:4

Why did God create sex? Why did He take one of the most complicated processes in the world—the creation of a child—and make it so simple that almost anyone could do it, without even taking a class in sex education? As I've looked through the Bible, I've found two reasons: through sex, God created a way to fulfill the desires of *His* heart, while at the same time fulfilling the desires of *our* hearts.

And what are the desires of His heart? We find out in the first words God spoke to the first couple on earth. You might be surprised that His first words to them were about sex, but they were! Take a look at what God said to Adam and Eve in the Garden of Eden:

"God blessed them and said to them, 'Be fruitful and increase in number; fill the earth and subdue it'" (Genesis 1:28a).

God told them to be fruitful and increase in number, and the way that people are fruitful is through sex.

Some people might think that the Bible is boring, but not the way I read it! Here in the opening scene you have two people, completely naked, standing in the middle of an exotic paradise, and the first thing their Creator says to them is, "Have at it! Be fruitful! Multiply!" Whew! If a movie came out this summer with an opening scene like that, teens and adults alike would line up around the block to go see it!

My wife Lana and I have taken those words to heart, and six kids later we're still having an awesome time fulfilling those first words that God spoke to the first people on the earth!

What do God's words to Adam and Eve tell us about the desires of His heart? On the surface, they tell us that He wants us to be fruitful and multiply. But why? Why does God *want* so many people?

Why? Because God *loves* people. He absolutely loves them, including you and me. God loves people so much that He wants the earth to be filled with them. One of the most famous verses in the Bible says, *"For God so loved the world..." (John 3:16a).*

God created sex for more than just to give Adam and Eve something to do on a Saturday night! God wanted them to be fruitful and multiply because He *loves* people and wants to have an intimate relationship with each and every one of us. God was so eager to see that you were born that He made it as easy and as attractive as possible for your parents to get together and create you.

The Desires of My Heart

But if you go back just a little further in the story of Adam and Eve, you'll see that God didn't create sex simply to fulfill the desires of *His* heart.

He also created sex in a way that it would fulfill the desires of *their* hearts.

The day I discovered that God wanted to fulfill Adam and Eve's desires was the same day I asked Lana to marry me.

Lana and I had met several years earlier when we both were in college together at the University of Illinois. But after we graduated, I moved to Texas and she moved to Michigan. A few years later, we wondered if God might want us to get back together again—this time for marriage. So Lana moved to Texas so that we could pray about the decision together. Early one Saturday morning, Lana came to my apartment and we went to watch a friend run a race. After the race, we came back to my apartment for some quiet time with God before going on with our day. Lana went to the living room with her Bible and I went to my bedroom with mine.

Just a few days earlier, I had finished reading through the entire Bible for the first time in my life, so I wasn't sure where to start reading again. I decided to start over from the beginning. I opened up to the first page of the first book of the Bible. I began to read about Adam, the first man on earth, and how God had set him in the Garden of Eden to work the land and take care of the animals. But in the midst of this beautiful setting, surrounded by all kinds of great things, God saw that Adam was still *alone:*

"The LORD God said, 'It is not good for the man to be alone. I will make a helper suitable for him'" (Genesis 2:18).

So God put Adam to sleep, took a rib from his side and created Eve, the first woman on earth. Then God brought her to Adam.

Even though I had heard this story since I was a kid, this was the first time I had seen it from *God's* perspective. As I read the story, my heart fell, as I'm sure God's must have fallen, when God saw how lonely Adam was. Then my heart rose again, as God's must have risen, when God created Eve and brought her to Adam. I'll bet the smile on Adam's face was about a mile wide!

As I pictured this scene in my mind, I suddenly had an intense awareness that God was looking down at me in the same way! There I was, surrounded by all kinds of great things, yet I was still *alone*. In that moment, God spoke to my heart in a way that went beyond words. He showed me that He had created a woman for me, too, and had brought her to me—right there in the next room! After months of praying, I finally knew that God really did want to fulfill the desires of my heart. He really did want me to marry Lana.

I ran down the hall to tell Lana what God had just told me. I didn't stop to look in the mirror as I ran, but if I did, I'll bet the smile on my face was about a mile wide! We talked, we cried, I asked her to marry me and she said, "Yes!"

When we were married a few months later, I discovered that God had fulfilled my desire for intimacy in a way that went beyond all I could ask or imagine. Sexual intimacy with my wife has become *the* most consistently exhilarating, off-the-charts experience of my life!

Throughout this book, I want to tell you not only how God has fulfilled the desires of *my* heart, but how God longs to fulfill the desires of *your* heart, too—because in doing so, God also fulfills the desires of *His* heart.

GOD'S TWIN PURPOSES FOR SEX

When you put these two scenes together from the life of Adam and Eve, you get a rich snapshot of God's twin purposes for creating sex:

- God wants us to be *intimate.*
- God wants us to be *fruitful.*
- Through sex, God has made a way for us to do both, *simultaneously.*

If you want to have the best possible sex life, you'll want to keep this snapshot at the forefront of your mind. At first glance, it may seem obvious that God created sex so that husbands and wives could be intimate and fruitful. But many people, myself included, have engaged in sex in ways that aren't obvious at all. Ways that don't lead to intimacy with *anyone,* let alone the husband or wife God has in mind for them. Ways that would *never* produce life. Ways that could even

17

lead to *death*—whether it's their own, someone else's, or the death of a child who has been unexpectedly conceived.

My hope with this book is to make the obvious...well, *obvious* again! I know how other things can cloud our minds to God's Truth, but I also know how God's Truth, when we honestly seek it, can break through and clear away the clouds.

I know that it wasn't until I discovered what God says about sex that I began to get a picture in my mind of the kind of sex life God had in store for me all along—one that He was still holding out for me if I was willing to take hold of it. One that He's still holding out for you, if you're willing to take hold of it, too.

GOD'S DESIRES FOR YOU

How does God's picture of an off-the-charts sex life line up with yours? How do God's hopes and dreams for your life line up with your hopes and dreams? Perhaps you even wonder if God *has* any hopes and dreams for your life? My prayer is that the truths that I've learned from

God's Word will help you to see that God *does* have hopes and dreams for your life, just as they've helped me, and many others, to see that God has hopes and dreams for our lives.

I'm excited for what God wants to share with you. In all the years that I've been applying these truths from God's Word to my sexual life, I've found that there is still no experience on earth that comes anywhere close to my sexual relationship with my wife.

The fact that you're reading this book at all makes me think that you want to experience this kind of abundant life, too—a life where your dreams and desires line up completely with God's. I believe you really want to do the "right thing," but I also know how hard it can be to know what the "right thing" is until someone speaks the truth with clarity.

Would you believe me if I told you that God wants to fulfill the desires of your heart even more than you want them fulfilled? That God really does have desires for your life that you may have only caught a glimpse of so far? In spite of sounding like a sensational headline on a check-out line magazine, it's true that God *really does* want you to have an awesome sex life! *He really is for you, not against you,* in your passionate pursuit of fulfilling the desires of your heart.

I'd like you to take a look at the review questions below. When you're done, we'll take a look at one of the *best* pieces of wisdom that God has ever given me regarding sex.

REVIEW QUESTIONS

1. *What were God's first words to the first couple on earth? (Genesis 1:28)*
2. *Why did God create Eve and bring her to Adam? (Genesis 2:18)*
3. *What are the twin purposes for which God created sex, as revealed in these two scenes?*
4. *Why would God want the world to be filled with people? (John 3:16)*

Staying Pure

"The man and his wife were both
naked, and they felt no shame."
Genesis 2:25

I n the very next sentence of Adam and Eve's story, God gives us one of the best pieces of wisdom for how to enjoy the best possible sex life:

"The man and his wife were both naked, and they felt no shame" (Genesis 2:25).

This is God's desire for every couple: that on their wedding day—when the ceremony is over and the guests have gone home—the bride and groom can take off their wedding clothes, with nothing to hide and with no sense of shame, and can finally become one flesh. Once they're married, God wants them to be able to continue to come together like this, naked and unashamed, over and over and over again.

While this may seem easy enough in concept, once our hormones kick in, triggering our God-given sexual desires, it can be a long and difficult wait until our wedding day. The wait is worth it, though, and God makes it clear that He not only *wants* us to wait, but He will *help* us to wait.

God's Protective Seal

In the days when Moses led the people of Israel out of Egypt, the Israelites had a marriage custom that proved whether or not a woman was a *virgin*—someone who has never had sex—on her wedding day.

When any woman has sex for the first time, the man's penis presses through a thin membrane of tissue, called the *hymen,* that partially covers the opening to her vagina. When the penis passes through the hymen for the very first time, a small amount of blood is produced as the hymen stretches open. This stretching occurs only once in a woman's lifetime, then the hymen remains fully open forever. The hymen acts like a protective seal on a medicine bottle: once the seal is broken, you know the bottle has already been opened.

In Moses' day, the newly married couple would save this first release of blood from the broken hymen on a piece of cloth. The cloth served as proof that the girl was indeed a virgin on her wedding day. If a man were to have sex with his new wife and find that there was no such sign of this proof, he had the right to bring her back to her father's house for swift and serious judgment. The law regarding this, as recorded in the Bible, says:

"If, however, the charge is true and no proof of the girl's virginity can be found, she shall be brought to the door of her father's house and there the men of her town shall stone her to death. She has done a disgraceful thing in Israel by being promiscuous while still in her father's house. You must purge the evil from among you" (*Deuteronomy 22:20-21*).

A man, too, was expected to be a virgin on his

wedding day. While a man's body has nothing comparable to the hymen that could break during sexual intercourse to prove his virginity, the Bible is just as clear that a man is not to have sex with anyone before marriage either, as described in detail in the rest of Deuteronomy 22.

(Please note that some women today do not bleed the first time they make love, especially those who have been active in sports or who have used tampons. Such activities can stretch the hymen prior to making love.)

While we no longer put people to death for breaking these laws, it's not because the laws are no longer *valid*, and not because the laws are no longer *valuable*. Thankfully, it's because when Jesus came to earth, He paid the price for our sins, including our sexual sins, so that whoever puts their faith in Him does not have to pay the penalty for their sins themselves, and is even able to live forever with Him. To finish the quote I began earlier about how much God loves people, the Bible says:

"For God so loved the world that he gave his one and

only Son, that whoever believes in him shall not perish but have eternal life" (John 3:16).

Jesus made it clear that while the law is still valid and valuable, He was willing to pay the penalty for our sins Himself, even the death penalty, because He loved us so much.

In a story that illustrates this, some people brought to Jesus a woman who had been caught in the act of *adultery*, which means she was having sex with someone else's husband. They asked Jesus if she should be punished and stoned to death according to the law or if she should be set free. The Bible says that the people were doing this to try to trap Jesus. His response revealed both His own brilliance and the wickedness of their hearts:

"If any one of you is without sin, let him be the first to throw a stone at her" (John 8:7b).

Amazingly, they all dropped their stones and left. They knew, as Jesus knew, that everyone has sinned at some point in their lives. Jesus also knew something that they didn't know: He knew that He Himself was about to pay the penalty for her sin, not to mention their sins, and yours and mine. The law was still valid and would soon be fulfilled by his death. But by taking her place and extending forgiveness, Jesus also extended her life, allowing her to fulfill the rest of the purposes for which God had created her in the first place. After all the other people had left the scene, Jesus asked the woman to turn away from the sins that almost got her killed:

"Woman, where are they? Has no one condemned you?"

"No one, sir," she said.

"Then neither do I condemn you," Jesus declared. "Go now and leave your life of sin" (John 8:10b-11).

God's expectations for, and the great value of, being sexually pure on our wedding day remains the same for us today as it was for the people in Moses' day. In order to have the best possible sex life within marriage, the first step is to *stay pure before marriage.* How can we do that? God tells us that, too.

A PIVOTAL CONVERSATION

A few months before I married Lana, I had a brief, but pivotal conversation with a man named John Smid, Executive Director of an organization called Love in Action. I had heard that John regularly counseled people regarding their sexual relationships, so I called him to ask about ways to safeguard my upcoming marriage so that it could be all that God wanted it to be.

Within the first few minutes of our conversation, I could tell that his words were going to be like nuggets of gold for my marriage. The first nugget appeared when he asked me about my current physical relationship with Lana. Did we kiss, hold hands and romantically touch each other in other ways? I told him we did. He then challenged me by asking me if she were someone else's wife, would I touch her in these ways? No, of course not! Then why, he asked, would I touch her in these ways before we got married? Because the truth was that until the day that we actually did get married, it was still possible that either of us could become someone else's husband or wife. Although I felt no hesitation about our commitment to our upcoming marriage, I knew that anything was possible and that John was telling me the truth.

A friend of ours told us recently about a sad situation involving her brother. He was engaged to be married to the girl of his dreams, but one month before the wedding, he succumbed to his temptations and had sex—not with the girl of his dreams, but with her sister, who had been unsuccessfully pursuing him for some time. Afterwards, he felt terrible about what he had just done, but his fiancé forgave him and they continued to plan for their wedding. Sadly, just days before the wedding, the sister discovered that she was pregnant with this man's baby. Torn between what he should do now, he married the girl's sister so that the child could have a father. Even more sadly, the sister then had a miscarriage shortly after the wedding, leaving the man in a marriage he hadn't planned on, leaving their unexpected child dead from the miscarriage, and leaving the girl of his dreams all alone. What a heartbreaking story, one that could have been avoided, even for two people who were "absolutely, positively" going to be married within a month. The truth is that we simply don't know what might happen prior to marriage.

Another woman wrote me to tell me that she and her boyfriend were living together, and although they weren't engaging in full sexual intercourse, they were, in her words, "simulating" sex. They hoped to get married sometime in the future, but not right now. She said she had heard that some Christians felt it was wrong to have this kind of sexual contact before marriage, but that she would need lots of explanation if this was wrong, because she craved the affection of her boyfriend and because she felt it was so natural to touch someone she loved.

Since I had just been shopping that day for a small rug for the entrance to our house, I used my shopping experience as an illustration to help her see the issue from God's perspective. Whenever I'd pull a rug off the shelf to see how it looked on the floor in the store, my two youngest sons would immediately start to walk on it. I kept having to tell them not to step on any of the rugs because they weren't ours yet. I didn't think someone else would want to buy a rug that had been walked on and soiled from other people's shoes. I know I wouldn't!

I told her that if that's how we're to treat a rug that's not yet ours, even though it is designed for being walked on, how should we treat someone else's precious and delicate body? If it's not ours, we shouldn't act as if it is, even if we're hoping it will become ours at some point. We wouldn't treat a rug as if it's ours until we went to the counter and paid for it properly, and we shouldn't treat another person as if they're ours until we walk down the aisle and commit our lives to each other "until death do us part." It is then—and only then—that we become husband and wife and *belong* to each other, as the Bible describes in the book of First Corinthians:

> *"The wife's body does not belong to her alone but also to her husband. In the same way, the husband's body does not belong to him alone but also to his wife" (1 Corinthians 7:4).*

WAITING TO AWAKEN LOVE

This sense of *belonging* to each other only comes within marriage between husbands and wives.

If this is the case, then where do we draw the line in our physical relationship with someone *before* marriage? The safest place to draw it is in the same place that we would draw it with someone else's husband or wife. Would I romantically kiss someone else's wife? Would I let my hand linger on her knee? Would I touch her breasts or her bottom, whether she were clothed or naked? Would I sexually stimulate her in any way, or let her do the same to me, whether it involved full sexual intercourse or just a "simulation" of the real thing? *Absolutely not!* And furthermore, would I want someone else to touch my future wife in these ways before I married her?

In one of the most romantic books in the Bible, the Song of Songs, one of the lovers in the book cautions repeatedly:

"Promise me, O women of Jerusalem, by the swift

31

gazelles and the deer of the wild, not to awaken love until the time is right" (Song of Songs 2:7b, and again in 3:5b and 8:4b, NLT).

God doesn't want us to even *awaken* romantic love until the time is right. Once love is aroused in a relationship, it is very difficult to back up again without tearing apart our hearts in the process.

I talked to another woman who was living with a man to whom she wasn't married. She told me that this man really treated her poorly, but that she had already gotten involved with him and didn't know how to get out of it. She asked me what to do. I told her, "Stop the relationship right now. Ask him to leave your house. Don't give your heart to someone who's not willing to commit to taking care of it for the rest of your life!" Her eyes were opened to what she was doing. Unfortunately, instead of stopping the relationship right then, it took her another month before she finally asked him to leave. In another sad turn of events, after he had finally left, she found out that she had become pregnant with his baby during their final month together. By the time she found out, the father was gone.

Please, don't do anything that would awaken love until the time is right.

This isn't to say that you can't give people a friendly hug or a "holy kiss" of greeting. But there's a big difference between a friendly hug or a holy kiss and a romantic, sexually arousing hug or kiss. Any activity that is sexually stimulating or arousing with anyone other than your husband or wife is unnecessary, unproductive and potentially damaging. You might ask, "What harm can it do?" That's a great question. Like the examples I've just given, it can do a lot of harm! But even if there weren't pregnancies or diseases to deal with, the damage that can be done to your heart is serious enough to warrant not "awakening love" with anyone but your husband or wife until "the time is right." One of the main regrets that people tell me they have about their sexual relationships prior to marriage is that they bring those memories into their marriage, memories that interfere with an otherwise beautiful relationship with their spouse, and which cannot be erased.

What harm can it do? Plenty. But there's still a better question: "What *good* can it do?" If engaging in sexual activities doesn't fulfill one of the twin purposes for which God created sex in the first place, to build intimacy or yield fruit with the husband or wife God has created for you, then it is more likely to be destructive to you or to others, whether now or down the road.

Not Even a Hint

There's no need to step on a rug to see if it's the one for you. You can, and should, look at it, admire it, and even carefully examine it before you commit to buying it, but you don't need to walk on it, soil it, or worse yet, muddy it up so much that no one else would even want it, which unfortunately happens in many sexual encounters.

Where, then, should we draw the line in our physical relationships? The Bible says that we should not have *even a hint* of sexual immorality among us:

"But among you there must not be even a hint of sexual

immorality, or of any kind of impurity, or of greed, because these are improper for God's holy people" (Ephesians 5:3).

My conversation with John Smid gave me new eyes regarding my relationship with Lana. Even though she and I were engaged to be married several months later and had already gone beyond the "hinting" stages in our physical relationship, I felt it was important that we pull back physically for those remaining months to the point where we physically treated one another as if we were someone else's husband or wife—because as remote as the possibility seemed, until our wedding day, there was still a chance that either of us *could* become someone else's husband or wife. It wasn't easy to keep our distance, and we weren't perfect at it, especially since we had already crossed those lines before. But I still saw the value in waiting to even *kiss* Lana again until that moment in the ceremony when the pastor finally said: "You may kiss the bride!"

And what an awesome moment that was when it finally came, to be able to kiss Lana, knowing that I would soon be able to fully embrace her, with all the rights and privileges that marriage gives to husbands and wives. By intentionally trying to refrain from even a hint of sexual immorality before marriage, it made the transition from singleness to marriage all the more sweet.

REVIEW QUESTIONS

1. *What did Adam and Eve* not *feel when they were first together, even though they were both naked? (Genesis 2:25)*
2. *In the days of Moses, what did the law say should be done if a man or woman had sex before marriage? (Deuteronomy 22:20-21, Deuteronomy 22:29)*
3. *Why do we no longer enact the punishments for these laws? Because they are no longer valid or valuable? Or because of some other reason? (John 8:1-11)*
4. *What does God* not *want us to have "even a hint of" in our lives? (Ephesians 5:3)*

3

DEALING WITH
TEMPTATION

*"But when you are tempted, he will also provide
a way out so that you can stand up under it."*
1 Corinthians 10:13b

dam and Eve were lucky, weren't they?
They didn't have to think about staying
pure before marriage. God just plopped
Eve onto Adam's lap, they knew they were meant
for each other, and God told them to be fruitful
and multiply!

How lucky can you get?

But staying pure isn't easy for any of us, even
for Adam and Eve.

In the next sentence of their story, Satan came
onto the scene and started asking questions: *"Did
God really say...?"*

This is one of Satan's most effective strategies
for taking us down: to get us to question what
God said—even though what God said may have

been perfectly clear at the time. God had told Adam that he could eat from any tree in the garden except one, because if he ate from it, he would die. Later, Satan simply asked them:

"Did God really say, 'You must not eat from any tree in the garden'?" (Genesis 3:1b).

Well, no, that's not what God *really* said (see Genesis 3), but it was enough to catch Adam and Eve off guard. They began to wonder if there might be a way around what God *really did* say in order to get what they wanted. Although initially they fought it, eventually they fell for it.

So did I.

GUESSING AT GOD'S INTENTIONS

Even though I grew up going to church, when I got to high school, I found myself torn between wanting to indulge my sexual desires and knowing that it wouldn't be right to do so. I began to give in, a little bit at a time. By the time I graduated from college, I was well down the road of sexual indulgence.

Lana followed a similar path. When she started dating, she wasn't quite sure where God wanted her to draw the line physically with the guys she was dating. As she would come to a new boundary line in her physical relationships, she would wonder if she should cross it or not. Each time she came back to the conclusion that God wanted her to be happy—and what she was doing made her really happy! So she guessed that what she was doing must be okay.

Lana and I both found out that once we were able to justify crossing one boundary, it was easier to cross the next. While the fear of pregnancy kept us both from engaging in full sexual intercourse with anyone before marriage, we didn't understand that the things we were doing were still setting us up for potential physical problems down the road—and guaranteed heartbreak—both of which could have been avoided.

Lana was right that God *did* want her to be happy! But the way to be truly happy is to be truly holy—staying pure in the eyes of God as well as your own. Like Adam and Eve found out, when we just *guess* at what God might say about how to be happy, instead of finding out what God really does say, we'll soon find that what we thought would make us happy is very short-lived —and can actually cause more unhappiness than we could have imagined.

TWO QUESTIONS

From our human point of view, some of the sexual activities in which people engage may not seem to be clear misuses of sex. But when we swirl around and take a look at them from God's viewpoint, the uses and misuses of sex become much more apparent.

We bought some dog treats one day to help train our new puppy. We thought they'd encourage her to do some things that were good for both her and us. We also had a toddler at the time who happened to find the treats! She started feeding them to the puppy one after another after another. Our puppy thought it was great! She got to eat all the treats she wanted! But how do you think it made us feel? We wanted the puppy to get the treats at some point—we obviously bought them for her—but the way in which she was getting them undermined the purpose for which we bought them in the first place.

God must feel the same way when we engage in sex in ways that don't fulfill His purposes for creating it. He wants us to enjoy the treat of sex at some point—He obviously designed it to be enjoyable for us—but He doesn't want us to engage in sex in ways which undermine the purposes for which He designed it in the first place.

The best way to stay pure before and within marriage is to swirl around and take a look at sex from God's point of view. You can usually see in a heartbeat if what you're doing is just for the sake of the treat, or for God's sake.

Here are two questions you can ask yourself to help decide if something you're doing, or considering doing, is in line with God's desires for you or not:

1) Will this lead to greater *intimacy* with the husband or wife God has created for me?

41

2) Will this lead to greater *fruitfulness* with the husband or wife God has created for me?

If any activity doesn't lead you into greater intimacy or fruitfulness with your spouse, it's more likely to destroy intimacy or fruitfulness.

A Way Out

I know how hard it can be to hold back from things that are sexually enticing. But as I mentioned before, God not only *wants* us to stay pure, He will also *help* us to stay pure.

Jesus is not some guy who's "out there" and who doesn't have a clue about the struggles we face. The Bible says this about Jesus, who is described here as our high priest:

"For we do not have a high priest who is unable to sympathize with our weaknesses, but we have one who has been tempted in every way, just as we are—yet was without sin" (Hebrews 4:15).

Jesus knows and understands what it's like to

be tempted. But He also shows us that God always provides us a way out of temptation.

I used to love to play a computer game called *Dark Castle*. The purpose was to try to escape from a castle in which you were trapped. Each room in the castle had a different challenge. Sometimes you had to throw rocks at bats, jump across moving stones, or duck out of the way of flying objects.

In each room there was something special to help you through it: a bag of rocks to throw, a special keystroke to help you jump higher, or a jet pack to help you fly. I would look around each room until I found the way of escape. When I found it, I would take it and move on to the next room. Eventually, I made it to the end. I defeated the enemy, escaped from the castle and was finally free.

God has promised that whenever we face a temptation, He has provided a way of escape. We may not always see it right away, or even *want* to see it, but it's *always* there. The Bible says:

> *"No temptation has seized you except what is common*

to man. And God is faithful; he will not let you be tempted beyond what you can bear. But when you are tempted, he will also provide a way out so that you can stand up under it" (1 Corinthians 10:13).

A friend of mine was traveling in another country when he was tempted to go into an area of a town that was known for all kinds of sexual activity. He said he just wanted to see what it was like. As he got onto the subway, he said a short prayer, asking God to provide a way out if God didn't want him to do this.

When the train stopped at his destination, he stepped onto the platform and was soon surrounded by a group of people who asked him to come with them. Although he had trouble understanding their language, he could tell they must be Christians and that they were inviting him to their church. Remembering his prayer, he decided to go with them instead of going to where he had originally planned. Amazingly, when he got to their church, they baptized him. They gave him a cup of hot tea and another subway ticket to get back home—which he promptly used for that purpose!

Of course, it would have been easier if my friend had simply *not* gotten on the train when he first thought about heading into sin. But the fact that God still answered his prayer and provided him yet another way out, is a demonstration of the lengths to which God will go to lead us out of temptation.

Jesus knew how real and significant our temptations would be. He knew that it was so important that He included it in His model prayer that He taught to His disciples to pray, which we now call the Lord's Prayer. It says, in part: *"And lead us not into temptation, but deliver us from the evil one"* *(Matthew 6:13)*.

The Apostle Paul felt that resisting temptation was so important that he wrote to the people living in Corinth: *"Flee from sexual immorality."* *(1 Corinthians 6:18a)*.

Joseph felt that fleeing from temptation was so important that when temptation came to him, he *ran* the other way! Take a look at what Joseph did when Potiphar's wife tried to seduce him: *"She*

45

caught him by his cloak and said, 'Come to bed with me!'
But he left his cloak in her hand and ran out of the
house." (Genesis 39:12). Joseph got thrown into jail
for running away, but jail was nothing compared
to the price he would have paid if he had stayed!
In the end, God honored Joseph's obedience and
made him second in command over all of Egypt.

When we're tempted, God *always* provides a
way of escape—even if it's just to turn and run—
and He wants us to take it every time.

LEARNING SELF-CONTROL

One of the best ways to deal with temptation
is to remove ourselves from its path as much as
possible. Although we can't eliminate all temptations, we have more control over them than we
might think.

I found this out for myself when I put into
practice something else that I learned from my
conversation with John Smid. After talking about
the way I treated *others* physically, the conversation turned to the way I treated *myself* physically.
John asked me whether or not I still *masturbated*,

which is a way of touching yourself that stimulates your sexual organs to an orgasm without having sexual intercourse with someone. I said that I did. Even though I had wondered what God thought of masturbation, I was never able to find enough evidence against it in the Bible to convince me to stop.

John told me that the reason he asked about masturbation wasn't so much about the issue of masturbation itself, but about the issue of self-control—because self-control *is* specifically mentioned in the Bible:

> *"It is God's will that you should be sanctified: that you should avoid sexual immorality; that each of you should learn to control his own body in a way that is holy and honorable, not in passionate lust like the heathen, who do not know God" (1 Thessalonians 4:3-5).*

John went on to say that he had found that masturbation was not only an issue for those who were single, but also for those who were married. If people regularly masturbated before they got married, they would usually continue to masturbate after they got married. The struggle over masturbation is not a struggle over sexual release, but a struggle over self-control.

When John interviewed several wives to ask what they would think if they knew their husbands were still masturbating after they got married, not one of the women responded with a positive view of it. The responses ranged from wondering what they, as wives, might be doing wrong sexually, to wondering what else their husbands might be doing if they weren't able to control themselves in this way.

Then John said something that inspired me: he told me that he—and many other people that he knew—had made a commitment to give up masturbation completely. Each of them could testify to the tremendous difference it had made in their lives. He had thrown down a *gauntlet*, a challenge that I had to decide whether or not I was going to pick up and apply to my own life.

I decided it was worth a try. So I made the commitment to myself and to Lana that I was going to try to give up masturbation completely, even before we got married. And as a way to hold myself accountable to that commitment, I told her that if I ever did give in to masturbation, I would confess it to her before the end of that same day.

I wish I could say I have been perfect in my resolve on this issue, too, but I can't! But I can say that I have kept my commitment to telling Lana before the day was out whenever I *have* given in. After just a few times of having to make that embarrassing confession, my resolve was set for good. This doesn't mean that the temptation has gone away or that I wouldn't like to give in to those temptations, but it does mean that my desire for self-control has overtaken my desire for giving in.

DRAWING A LINE IN THE HEART

That one decision has kept me pure in more ways than one over the years.

When I happened to run into John Smid again, sixteen years later, I showed him a picture of my family, which was still just a glimmer in my eye at the time when we had first talked. I thanked him for the nuggets of truth he had shared with me and told him about how my my decision to stop masturbating had kept me pure in other ways, too.

Gaining control over masturbation has kept me from other sexual activities that are more serious and are clearly condemned in Scripture, such as:

- *Adultery,* which involves sex with someone who isn't your husband or wife, and is listed as one of the top Ten Commandments: *"You shall not commit adultery" (Exodus 20:14).*
- *Prostitution,* which involves paying someone to have sex with you: *"Do you not know that your bodies are members of Christ himself? Shall I then take the members of Christ and unite them with a prostitute? Never! Do you not know that he who unites himself with a prostitute is one with her in body? For it is said, 'The two will become one flesh'" (1 Corinthians 6:15-16).*
- and *Pornography,* which involves looking at things like books, magazines, pictures, tapes, or movies that are designed to arouse you

sexually. Jesus said: *"You have heard that it was said, 'Do not commit adultery.' But I tell you that anyone who looks at a woman lustfully has already committed adultery with her in his heart"* (Matthew 5:27-29).

A question people often ask is, "How far can I go?" meaning, "How far can I go with someone physically before God considers it a sin?" It's a common question, but I think it's the wrong question. Jesus, in his quote about adultery, reveals that the sin doesn't occur just when we cross a physical boundary, but when we cross a boundary in our heart. The best place to draw the line is not in the flesh, but in the heart, because once a line has been crossed in the heart, it's that much easier to cross it in the flesh. The Bible explains how these *wrongful desires of our heart* can lead us into *wrongful actions,* which can lead to *destruction:*

"When tempted, no one should say, 'God is tempting me.' For God cannot be tempted by evil, nor does he tempt anyone; but each one is tempted when, by his own

evil desire, he is dragged away and enticed. Then, after desire has conceived, it gives birth to sin; and sin, when it is full-grown, gives birth to death" (James 1:13-15).

Tim Wilkins, Executive Director of Cross Ministry, which also helps people overcome their sexual struggles, tells this helpful story for dealing with temptation:

An affluent, aristocratic woman reviews resumés from potential chauffeurs to drive her Rolls Royce. She narrows the applicants to three men and invites them to her palatial home.

She escorts each one individually to her driveway and the brick wall beside it.

She asks, "If you were driving my Rolls, how close do you think you could come to that brick wall without scratching my car?"

The first applicant says, "I can drive within a foot of that wall and not damage your Rolls."

She brings out the second applicant and asks, "If you were driving my Rolls, how close do you think you could come to that brick wall without scratching my car?"

He scratches his head and says, "I can drive within six inches of that wall and not damage your car."

She invites the third applicant and asks, "If you were driving my Rolls, how close do you think you could come to that brick wall without scratching my car?"

He does not hesitate, "Ma'am, I do not know how close I could come to the wall without damaging your car, but if I was driving your car, I would stay as far away as possible from the wall so as not to damage your car."

Guess who got the job?

Tim adds, "When addressing sexual temptation, the point is not how close one can get to the temptation without getting 'scratched,' but staying as far away as possible. *'Keep to a path far from her, do not go near the door of her house...' (Proverbs 5:8)."*

For me, by drawing a line in the sand way back at masturbation, I have been able to keep from being drawn into activities that are further down the road and that could be much more destructive to God's desires—and my desires—for my life and my marriage. It has helped me to keep my thoughts in check, knowing that there's no need to linger on a tempting thought for more than a moment because I know I won't be following through on that thought, even if it were "only" through masturbation.

John Smid said that he continues to recommend that people give up masturbation, especially if they struggle with other sexual temptations, for two reasons: 1) because it builds a person's confidence in their ability to gain control over their own body, and 2) because even if they do occasionally fail in this struggle, the results are not as devastating as if they fall into more serious temptations.

This one nugget of truth, related to controlling our bodies and based on the Word of God, has saved me, my wife and my family from a lifetime of grief. No wonder I love the Bible so much!

The Bible takes the guesswork out of wondering what God says about sex. In the next chapter, I'll share the first thing I read in the Bible as an adult regarding sex, something which turned out to be one of the most significant turning points of my life.

REVIEW QUESTIONS

1. *What is one of Satan's most effective strategies to get us to sin? (Genesis 3:1)*
2. *What two questions can you ask yourself to help determine if a sexually stimulating activity is in line with God's purposes or not?*
3. *When you are tempted to sin, what does God say He will always do for you? (1 Corinthians 10:13)*
4. *What does God want us to learn to control? (1 Thessalonians 4:3-5)*

BECOMING
PURE AGAIN

*"If we confess our sins, he is faithful and just and will
forgive us our sins and purify us from all unrighteousness."
1 John 1:8-9*

Your purity matters so much to God that He's made a way for you to become pure again—even if you mess up. And at some point in our lives, we all mess up!

God isn't surprised when we sin. None of us have a perfect moral scorecard, from Adam and Eve all the way down to you and me. When we do sin, most of us feel what Adam and Eve felt:

"At that moment, their eyes were opened, and they suddenly felt shame at their nakedness. So they strung fig leaves together around their hips to cover themselves. Toward evening they heard the LORD God walking about in the garden, so they hid themselves among the

trees. The LORD God called to Adam, 'Where are you?'
He replied, 'I heard you, so I hid. I was afraid because I was naked'" (Genesis 3:7-10, NLT).

When we sin, we feel naked and ashamed, trying to cover our nakedness and then running away from God. But that's the time we most need to run *back* to God. He wants to restore us to purity again. God loved Adam and Eve too much to leave them alone. He went looking for them, just as He goes looking for us because of His great love for us.

"But God demonstrates his own love for us in this: While we were still sinners, Christ died for us" (Romans 5:8).

If you find yourself feeling naked and ashamed of your sin, you don't have to run away. Just turn around. You'll find that God has been running after you and is eager to take you back and make you pure again.

The same Bible that shows us how to have the

best possible sex life is the same Bible that shows us how to be forgiven when we fall short of God's best.

FALLING INTO SIN

I didn't realize how far I had strayed from what God says about sex until the year after I got out of college and began to read the Bible for myself. The more I read, the more I realized that the things I had done sexually were wrong in God's eyes—and could even destroy my life if I continued to do them. I began to see that the bad choices that I had made, and the sins that I had committed, might actually cause my own death. I was especially struck by a verse in the Bible that clarified for me that if I *did* die, I would simply be reaping the consequences of my own sinfulness, the *wages*—or what I had earned for my sin:

"For the wages of sin is death, but the gift of God is eternal life in Christ Jesus our Lord" (Romans 6:23).

When I saw that these words applied specifically to *my* life, I decided to take a long walk with God along a bayou that ran through downtown Houston.

As I walked, I wondered if some of the things I had done sexually might have already done irreparable damage to my body through sexual diseases I might have contracted. I had never given it much thought before, but after reading what the Bible said about the natural consequences of sin, I knew that it was quite possible that I would eventually reap what I had sown.

At the same time, I was starting to see that God really did have a plan for the world, and more specifically, for my life, too. I realized that my sins would not only bring me down, but would also bring down the plans God had for my life. I could see that God had a better path in mind for me than the one I was on, and I wanted more than anything to find out how to get onto it.

But how? How could I undo what I had already done? How could I change my wrongful thoughts, feelings and desires? How could I change the habits that I had fallen into that were still threatening to destroy me?

As if in answer to my questions, I ran across another story in the Bible—the story of two blind men who came to Jesus to be healed. I was carrying my Bible with me as I walked along the bayou, reading from the book of Matthew. I was intrigued by Jesus' words in response to the pleas of the blind men. They called out to Jesus, *"Have mercy on us, Son of David!" (Matthew 9:27b).* In other places in the Bible, Jesus healed people by bending down to make a paste of mud to put on their eyes, or by telling them to dip in a certain pool of water. But not with these two. Jesus asked them a question:

"Do you believe that I am able to do this?" (Matthew 9:28b).

Based on their answer, Jesus would or would not heal them.

I wanted Jesus to heal me of my wrongful sexual desires and actions, just like the blind men asked Him to heal their eyes. I felt like He was asking me the same question: "Eric, do you believe that I am able to do *this*, too?" I thought about everything I had ever learned about Jesus: how He healed the sick, walked on water and raised the dead. I knew that if anyone could do it, Jesus could.

I stopped along the path and put my hand up into the air. Just like the blind men, I answered, *"Yes, Lord."* And just like the blind men, Jesus healed me:

> *"Then he touched their eyes and said, 'According to your faith will it be done to you,' and their sight was restored"* (Matthew 9:29-30a).

I knew in that moment that I had been healed. It was as distinct as if I had been blind and now could see. The next day I put my faith in Christ for everything in my life, asking Him to forgive me of my sins, and receiving from Him the gift of eternal life. Doing this turned out to be the turning point for the rest of my life.

DAVID'S TURNING POINT

If you've ever sinned, you're in good company

—or at least *a lot* of company. We all share this common trait.

The Bible says, *"...for all have sinned and fall short of the glory of God" (Romans 3:23)*, and *"We all, like sheep, have gone astray, each of us has turned to his own way..." (Isaiah 53:6a)*.

Sin—of any kind—does more to short-circuit the abundant life God has for us than perhaps anything else. Sexual sin seems to be especially devastating. Why? The Bible says,

"Flee sexual immorality. All other sins a man commits are outside his own body, but he who sins sexually, sins against his own body" (1 Corinthians 6:18).

But God has given us a way to overcome a short-circuit to bring us back to full power again: through *confession*.

To confess means "to agree with," to recognize that what we've done is wrong with a desire to make it right again. Confession is what David expressed to God when his sin with Bathsheba finally caught up to him.

You might remember that David was one of

the greatest kings of all time, but that he fell into sexual sin with Bathsheba, a woman who was married to another man. When David looked out from his palace and saw her bathing naked on her roof, he wanted her. He asked her to come to him and fell to one of the lowest points of his life. He might have remained at that point until the day he died except that God, through one of David's counselors, confronted David about his sin. When David realized what he had done, he poured out his heart in confession to God.

David's words are recorded in Psalm 51:

> *"Have mercy on me, O God, according to your unfailing love; according to your great compassion blot out my transgressions. Wash away all my iniquity and cleanse me from my sin. For I know my transgressions, and my sin is always before me. ... Cleanse me with hyssop, and I will be clean; wash me, and I will be whiter than snow. ... Create in me a pure heart, O God, and renew a steadfast spirit within me" (Psalm 51:1-3, 7, 10).*

David and Bathsheba, and those around them, paid a price for their sin. Bathsheba's husband died when David had him killed in the cover-up attempt. Then the son born to David and Bathsheba died soon after his birth. To top it all off, their sin was recorded in the Bible for all time for all of us to see.

But all was not lost. Because David confessed his sin and turned back to God, God did for David what he asked: God cleansed him, washed him, and made him whiter than snow. God gave him a pure heart again and renewed his spirit. David married Bathsheba and they conceived another son. That son, Solomon, went on to become one of the richest and wisest kings in all of history. The turning point in David's life hinged on David's confession to God and his cry to make things right again.

It's the same turning point that can determine the outcome of our future, too.

THE POWER OF CONFESSION

I met with a couple one night to pray that they would be able to have a child. They had wanted one for years but were unable to conceive. The doctor had finally declared the wife *infertile*, meaning she would never be able to have children.

Before I prayed with them, I asked them to tell me a little more about what they were going through and what they wanted God to do for them. It turned out that there was more to their story than infertility. Soon after they were married, they discovered they had a *sexually transmitted disease,* or *STD.* STD's are usually only passed from person to person by sexual contact. This particular STD was terribly painful—each time they made love, it would flare up again and cause one or the other of them pain in their sexual organs.

They didn't know how they had gotten the STD, or who had brought it into the relationship, because each of them had been sexually active with others before they were married. But the result was that it lead them both to an underlying hurt and resentment that hadn't gone away.

Before praying for their fertility, I led them in a time of prayer and confession to each other of their past actions and their present hurts that were brought on by their sin. The healing that

God performed in their hearts was immediately visible on their faces, as they beamed with forgiveness and a new appreciation of each other. By the time we got to praying for their fertility, there was little left to do but to simply ask God to heal their bodies as well.

Over the next few months, the husband called me several times to tell me what a huge difference those prayers had made in their marriage, including their sex life. Just over a year later, this "infertile" couple gave birth to a child—the fruit of their renewed intimacy. Although they still carried within their bodies the disease from their former sin, God found a way to bypass that condition and continue on with His plan for their lives—and for the life of their child.

Our prayers of confession are powerful. They have a real and practical effect. But they're not a "magic formula" that help us get whatever we want. In fact, the couple I mentioned above wanted more children after the birth of their first, but they've not been able to conceive again. There are many factors that can contribute to how our prayers may or may not be answered, which is why continual prayers for wisdom and continual trust in God is important regardless of the outcome. But confession *can* be one of the things that can bring us the healing we need to move on with God's plans for our lives. The Bible says,

> *"Therefore confess your sins to each other and pray for each other so that you may be healed. The prayer of a righteous man is powerful and effective"* (James 5:16).

I've seen this same pattern repeat over and over as I've talked with other people who have been at an impasse in their sexual lives. They often see a breakthrough when they finally confess their sins, first to God, and then to their spouse.

A man who had struggled with pornography and illicit chat rooms for years confessed his sin to me. We prayed through it together, seeking God's forgiveness for what he had done. I then encouraged him to confess it to his wife, as his sin had affected their sexual relationship, too. Although the husband was fearful to confess it to her, he did. When she forgave him, he was finally free, not only from the pornography that had gripped him, but free to to love his wife intimately again.

Another man confessed to me that he had struggled with true intimacy with his wife for years. He told me some of the personal struggles in his life that he had never shared with his wife for fear that she would leave him. I encouraged him that in order to break through to the true intimacy he wanted with his wife, he needed to confess those things to her. With much fear and trepidation, he did. His wife was shocked, went for a walk, and prayed. When she came back, she told him: "I still love you." He later told me, "Eric, she's told me thousands of times that she loved me, but this was the first time that I've ever really believed her."

God is in the life-changing business. He's been turning people's lives around from sexual sin for thousands of years. Read what the Apostle Paul wrote in a letter to the Christians in the church of Corinth about 2,000 years ago:

"Do you not know that the wicked will not inherit the

*kingdom of God? Do not be deceived: Neither the
sexually immoral nor idolaters nor adulterers nor male
prostitutes nor homosexual offenders nor thieves nor the
greedy nor drunkards nor slanderers nor swindlers will
inherit the kingdom of God. And that is what some of
you were. But you were washed, you were sanctified,
you were justified in the name of the Lord Jesus Christ
and by the Spirit of our God" (1 Corinthians 6:9-11).*

There's a little word in there that says a lot:
it's the little verb *were.* "And that is what some of
you *were.*" They struggled with all kinds of sins,
but they didn't stay that way. They were changed,
transformed, and made new again, just like I was.
Although there are consequences for our sin,
some of which can last a lifetime, none are so serious that they can't be washed, sanctified and justified in the name of the Lord Jesus Christ and by
the Spirit of our God.

GOD-GIVEN PURITY

Confession is more than just good for the soul.

It's good for finally living the life for which God created you to live.

If you're wrestling with unconfessed sin in your life, I want to encourage you to prayerfully consider when, where and to whom to confess it. While it may seem terrifying to admit your sins to God and to the ones you love, the truth is that God already knows about them—and the ones you love are probably already feeling the effects of them. Finally confessing them will help to identify the source so that things can begin to change.

None of us are without sin, but none of us are beyond God's forgiveness either. Whenever we confess our sins to Him, He promises to forgive us and make us pure again.

"If we claim to be without sin, we deceive ourselves and the truth is not in us. If we confess our sins, he is faithful and just and will forgive us our sins and purify us from all unrighteousness" (1 John 1:8-9).

If you ever find yourself in need of a prayer of confession and don't know what to say, here are a few words to help you get started. One heartfelt prayer can be the turning point of your life, too.

Father, I'm sorry for the sins I've committed against You and against others. I know I can't make up for these sins, but I know that Jesus has already paid the price for them when He died on the cross. I am putting my full faith and trust in Jesus right now and I ask Him to be the Lord of my life. Fill me with Your Holy Spirit so that I can be washed, cleansed, purified, and made righteous again in Your sight. I pray this all in Jesus' name, Amen.

REVIEW QUESTIONS

1. *What did God do to demonstrate His love for us, even while we were still sinning? (Romans 5:8)*
2. *What question did Jesus ask the blind men when they wanted to be healed? (Matthew 9:28)*
3. *What is one thing James says we can do so that we may be healed? (James 5:16)*
4. *What does God promise to do if we confess our sins to Him? (1 John 1:8-9)*

5

KNOWING
YOUR SPOUSE

*"Now Adam knew Eve and
she conceived and bore Cain."
Genesis 4:1, NKJV*

You may have heard about the group of scientists who got together and decided that man had come a long way and no longer needed God.

They picked one scientist to go and tell Him that they were done with Him. The scientist walked up to God and said, "God, we've decided that we no longer need You. We're to the point that we can clone people and do many miraculous things, so why don't You just go on and get lost."

God listened patiently to the man and when the scientist was done talking, God said, "Very well! How about this? Let's have a man-making contest."

To which the man replied, "Okay, great!"

But God added, "Now we're going to do this just like I did back in the old days with Adam."

The scientist said, "Sure, no problem," and bent down and grabbed himself a handful of dirt.

God just looked at him and said, "No, no, no. You go and get your own dirt!"

We may think that our new reproductive technologies are remarkable, like *artificial insemination,* where a man's sperm and a woman's eggs are extracted from their bodies and then coaxed together in a test tube. Or *cloning,* where scientists take a few cells from one body and try to fuse them together with an egg from another body, and then try to spark life into them by using an electric shock in a sterile lab. These technologies *are* remarkable, but compared to the way God designed sex to create a new life in the first place, there's no doubt in my mind which process is *more* remarkable—and more fun!

Given the choice, I think most people would rather create a new life the old-fashioned way: by making love, not just making babies. The reason for this goes deeper than just the fact that love-making can be tremendously fun.

YADA!

The reason is that God wants us to *know* our husband or wife, deeply and intimately, and making love with them is one of the deepest ways we can know them.   In fact, one of the Hebrew words that is often used in the Bible to describe making love is *yada,* which literally means "to know."

For instance, the Bible says:

"Now Adam knew Eve and she conceived and bore Cain" (Genesis 4:1; see also Genesis 4:17, 1 Samuel 1:19, NKJV).

To *know* someone, in the biblical sense, means to have sexual intercourse with them.   An easy way to remember what the word *intimacy* means is to think of the phrase "into-me-see."   When we're intimate with our husband or wife, we're allowing them to see into us and they're allowing us to see into them.

Why does God want you to *know* your spouse so intimately? Because God wants you to use your hands, your eyes, your words, your ears, your heart—your whole being—to express *His* love to them, as well as your own.

As much as God wants to fulfill the desires of *your* heart, He also wants to fulfill the desires of *your spouse's* heart—through you! In order to do that effectively, it's vitally important that you know your spouse, deeply and intimately, so that you can touch them in the way God wants them to be touched.

WHY DON'T YOU MARRY HER?

The first time this struck me, that God wanted to work through me to fulfill the desires of Lana's heart, started before I even thought about marrying her.

Lana was still living in Michigan and I was living in Texas. Even though we had dated in college, we had broken up two years earlier, but we still talked on the phone from time to time. One night, Lana told me that she was wondering if God wanted her to stay at her current job or not. I told her that I was planning a special time of prayer and fasting that week, so I'd pray about her job decision, too.

By day two of my fast, I was feeling spiritually stronger, but a little lightheaded. I was sitting by a pool in the warm Texas sun, having taken the day off work to pray. When I began praying for Lana, I didn't picture her wearing a suit and tie, working for a large corporation for the rest of her life—I pictured her at home, married and raising a family.

That's it, Lord! She doesn't need a different job. What she needs is a husband who will take care of her so that she can stay home. I began to pray that God would bring her a husband.

Then these words floated through my mind as clear as the water in front of me: "Why don't *you* marry her?"

What?!? That's not what I was praying about at all! Maybe the fast was affecting me more than I thought!

But two weeks later, even after my fast was over, the question was still at the forefront of my mind: "Why don't *you* marry her?"

I began to ask myself the same thing: "Why *don't* I marry her?" It wasn't that I didn't like her. In fact, when we dated in college, I was totally in love with her. But the reason we broke up two years earlier was because God had already been working on my heart and I felt He was the one prompting me to break up with her. At the time, I didn't even know why God would want us to break up. But in the months following our breakup, both of us decided to put our faith in Christ. We then began to learn what God says about sex and realized that what we had been doing was wrong.

Now, two years later, and having both given our lives to Christ, maybe God really *did* want us to get back together! I had to find out, one way or the other, so I decided to set aside the next three months to pray and see if this question was really from God or not. Lana and I still talked from time to time, but I didn't tell her about my prayers, both for her sake and for my own. I just wanted to hear clearly from God without the pressure of a relationship.

Over those next few months, God put a love in my heart for Lana that surpassed anything I had ever felt before. I was able to listen to her from a distance and see how she felt on issues that were important to me, her relationship with Christ, and her dreams and desires. I tried to look at her the way God looks at her to see if I could really meet her needs the way God wanted them to be met.

By the end of the three months of praying, I was about ready to burst! I was so in love with her that I told God I'd be *really* mad at Him if He *didn't* let me marry her!

KNOWING YOUR SPOUSE BEFORE MARRIAGE

God cares deeply about who we marry. I don't know whether or not God has prearranged, from the beginning of time, who He wants us to marry. But I do know that He has a definite stake in the decision.

There are certain things that God wants us to

know about our spouse even before we marry them. In several places in the Bible, God gives us clear guidelines, as well as specific guidance, about the person He wants us to marry.

I remember when our first two kids were younger, they wondered if they could marry each other when they grew up. I'm glad they liked each other so much at the time to even think of it, but we said, "No, God will give you someone else to marry."

How did we know this and they didn't? Because we knew it was against the law and they didn't, and also because we had read it in the Bible and they hadn't. Some of the things we take for granted are obvious to us only because we, or someone before us, has discovered them in God's Word. Here are a few of the general guidelines that God gives in the Bible for who He wants us to marry—and *not* marry.

- God wants believers in Christ to marry other believers: *"Do not be yoked together with unbelievers, for what do righteousness and wickedness have in common?" (2 Corinthians 6:14a)*.

- God doesn't want us to marry someone who would turn our hearts away from Him: *"You must not intermarry with them [those who serve other gods], because they will surely turn your hearts after their gods"* (1 Kings 11:2b).
- God tells us who is off-limits for sexual relations, and therefore off limits for marriage:
  - We're not to have sexual relations with any close relative: *"No one is to approach any close relative to have sexual relations. I am the LORD"* (Leviticus 18:6). In the same chapter, God then goes on to define close relatives as our parents, children, brothers and sisters, grandparents, grandchildren, aunts and uncles, and nieces and nephews;
  - We're not to have sexual relations with anyone who is already married, which would be *adultery*; *"Do not have sexual relations with your neighbor's wife and defile yourself with her"* (Leviticus 18:20);
  - Nor with animals, which is called *bestiality*: *"Do not have sexual relations with an ani-*

mal and defile yourself with it" (Leviticus 18:23a);

~ Nor with people who are the same sex as us, which is called *homosexuality* among men and *lesbianism* among women: *"Do not lie with a man as one lies with a woman; that is detestable"* (Leviticus 18:22) and *"Because of this, God gave them over to shameful lusts. Even their women exchanged natural relations for unnatural ones. In the same way the men also abandoned natural relations with women and were inflamed with lust for one another. Men committed indecent acts with other men, and received in themselves the due penalty for their perversion"* (Romans 1:26-27).

Those in the Bible who ask for God's input about who to marry are invariably blessed, such as Isaac and Rebekah (see Genesis 24) and Jacob and Rachel (see Genesis 29). Those who don't follow God's advice invariably pay the price, such as Amnon and Tamar (see 2 Samuel 13:1-21) and Solomon and his foreign wives (see 1 Kings 11:1-4).

This is not to say that God can't redeem and restore any marriage—because He can and He has! I've seen Him do it several times! But those who have gone into marriage without listening first to what God says will be the first ones to tell you that they wished they had followed God's advice.

God cares who you marry because He cares about you, He cares about your spouse, and He cares about the children who may result from your marriage.

A Gift From God

During those three months that I prayed about marrying Lana, I was able to find out several things about her. I could see that she was a believer and that she would encourage me in my walk with the Lord, not turn me away from Him. I already knew she wasn't a close relative, she wasn't married, she wasn't an animal, and she wasn't a man. So far so good!

When my three months of prayer came to an end, I decided to call Lana and tell her everything that was on my heart. When we started talking, she told me she had finally decided to quit her job. She knew it was the right thing to do, but she didn't know what she was going to do next. I told her I had an idea!

When I asked her to consider moving to Houston so we could pray together about possibly getting married, she was the one that went into shock! *What?!?* she thought. *That's not what I was praying about at all!*

Now she needed some time to pray about it. During those next few months, there was nothing I could do but wait. At one point during this time, when I honestly didn't know what Lana might decide, I read this passage in the Bible:

"May he give you the desire of your heart and make all your plans succeed. We will shout for joy when you are victorious and will lift up our banners in the name of our God. May the LORD grant all your requests" (Psalm 20:4-5).

Once again, the words of the Bible seemed to leap off the page. I knew in that moment that

Lana was the desire of my heart. Although I knew it might sound like a childish prayer, I said, "Lord, You've already given me more than I deserve by forgiving my sins and giving me eternal life with You. But if I could ask you for only one gift the rest of my life, it would be to marry Lana." I had no idea if God would grant me my request, and I was willing to trust Him whatever the outcome, but I also knew that I would "shout for joy," as it said in Psalm 20, if He did let me marry her!

Less than a year later, as we were standing at the altar exchanging our wedding vows, I looked at Lana with tears in my eyes and a lump in my throat and said, "Lana, ever since I read Psalm 20 that said, *May He give you the desire of your heart'* I've known that you are the desire of my heart. ... You are a gift from God to me, and I plan to treat you as a gift."

MAKING LOVE

A husband or wife really is a gift from God— and God wants us to treat them as gifts. That includes the way we treat them sexually. One of the problems with sex is that people often use it to get what they want, rather than to give what God wants. *Making love* is more than just another term for sex, it also describes *the way* we should do it.

There are times when I'll look at Lana and ask myself, *If God were here right now, what would He do to bless her?* How would *He* want me to use my hands, my words, my eyes, my ears, and my heart to bless her in a special way? Sometimes I'll sense that God wants me to caress her forehead, stroke her hair, or give her gentle kisses on her lips and cheeks. While it's nearly impossible for me not to take pleasure in this, too, my honest motivation at times like these is not to satisfy my own desires, but to let God work through me to satisfy hers. I usually find that by blessing her, God uses her to bless me back!

By knowing our spouse, deeply and intimately, we can better minister to their needs. The Bible says that husbands and wives ought to care for each other's bodies as if they were their own:

"In this same way, husbands ought to love their wives as their own bodies. He who loves his wife loves himself. After all, no one ever hated his own body, but he feeds and cares for it, just as Christ does the church—for we are members of his body" (Ephesians 5:28-30).

Ironically, some people will joke with their spouse when they don't want to have sex by saying, "Not tonight, honey, I have a headache." But in reality, sex might be just what the doctor ordered. I've been amazed that throughout our married life, whenever my wife really does have a headache, godly caressing and lovemaking has brought about the complete and total cure! God has been able to work through me to bring about the healing she needs.

I'd like to give you a short list of suggestions for how to truly make love with your spouse, all of which revolve around *knowing* your spouse.

1) *Treat one another with love and respect.* God wants to use our hands, our bodies and our words to express *His* love to our spouses, not in any way that is hurtful or disrespect-

ful. Does this delight my spouse? Does it make them feel truly loved and respected? Does it make them feel appreciated and genuinely cared for? *"However, each one of you also must love his wife as he loves himself, and the wife must respect her husband"* (Ephesians 5:33).

2) *Build each other up, not tear each other down.* Some types of touching may be exciting to us, but may cause physical or emotional harm to our spouse or to ourselves. God has wired our bodies to sense pain so that we can tell when something needs extra care. *"Love is patient, love is kind. It does not envy, it does not boast, it is not proud. It is not rude, it is not self-seeking, it is not easily angered, it keeps no record of wrongs. Love does not delight in evil but rejoices with the truth. It always protects, always trusts, always hopes, always perseveres"* (1 Corinthians 13:4-7).

3) *Make love regularly.* The Bible doesn't give us a "norm" for how often a married couple should engage in sex, but it does say that we

should not deprive each other of these times of intimacy, except when both spouses agree and only for a limited time. Ask God what *He* wants you to do for your spouse, inviting His Holy Spirit into your lives to help you find what may even be creative ways to bless them. *"The husband should fulfill his marital duty to his wife, and likewise the wife to her husband. The wife's body does not belong to her alone but also to her husband. In the same way, the husband's body does not belong to him alone but also to his wife. Do not deprive each other except by mutual consent and for a time, so that you may devote yourselves to prayer. Then come together again so that Satan will not tempt you because of your lack of self-control"* (1 Corinthians 7:3-5).

4) *Take time to learn the differences between your own body and your spouse's.* While most men can be aroused and have an orgasm within just a few minutes, it takes most women twenty minutes or more to have an orgasm. While a man may be ready to engage in full sexual

intercourse within the first few minutes, he would find his wife is much more receptive after taking twenty minutes or more to just talk and touch and caress her until she is ready, too. I shared this simple fact with a friend before his wedding and when he came back from his honeymoon, he said that knowing this fact had made all the difference in the way he approached sex with his new wife and their mutual experience of it. If there's one book about sex that I would recommend to you so that you can learn more about your spouse and godly lovemaking, it would be Dr. Ed and Gaye Wheats' book, *Intended For Pleasure.*

5) *Recognize the unique way God created humans to make love.* Did you know that human beings are the only creatures that can engage in sexual intercourse face-to-face? This is one of many facts I learned from the Wheats' book that has helped me to appreciate even more the way God created our bodies to relate sexually. While many books about sex

go into great detail about various sexual positions a couple might try, don't think it's a small thing to make love in one of the most obvious positions of all—face-to-face with your husband or wife, a position that God has reserved for humans alone.

6) *Pray for each other daily.* One simple thing that Lana and I have done since the beginning of our marriage is to go to bed together at the same time whenever we can, and to pray for each other, out loud, every night before going to sleep. This has helped us to know each other even better, as we share about the important things in our lives needing prayer. It allows us to cover each other in prayer, as well as to regularly "clear the air" if there has been any tension between us during the day, as the Bible encourages all of us to do: *"Do not let the sun go down while you are still angry..." (Ephesians 4:26b).* This time of spiritual intimacy is often a precursor to a time of physical intimacy.

Our lovemaking can and should be life-giving, not destructive in any way. As Jesus said:

"The thief [Satan] comes only to steal and kill and destroy; I have come that they may have life, and have it to the full" (John 10:10).

By knowing your spouse, deeply and intimately, this can be yet another way that you can experience just such a full and abundant life. And as you'll see in the next chapter, it can bring about an abundance of life in other ways, too!

REVIEW QUESTIONS

1. What is the meaning behind the Hebrew word "yada" which the Bible uses to describe sexual relations? (as used in Genesis 4:1, NKJV)

2. Who are some of the people listed in the Bible with whom God does not want us to engage in sexual relations or marriage? (2 Corinthians 6:14, 1 Kings 11:2, Leviticus 18)

3. How does God want husbands and wives to treat each other's bodies? (Ephesians 5:28-30)

4. *What are some additional ways that God wants us to treat each other that can also be applied to sexual intimacy? (Ephesians 5:33, 1 Corinthians 13:4-7, 1 Corinthians 7:3-5)*

6

VIEWING CHILDREN AS BLESSINGS

"God blessed them and said to them,
'Be fruitful and increase in number.'"
Genesis 1:28

I f God wanted to bless you, what do you think those blessings might look like? Don't be surprised if they actually look a little bit like *you!*

For Adam and Eve, whom the Bible says were the first people that God "blessed," God told them what form their blessing would take: *"God blessed them and said to them, 'Be fruitful and increase in number'" (Genesis 1:28).* God could have blessed them and said, "Here, have four or five vacation homes!" or "Here, have nine or ten priceless cars!" But instead He blessed them and said, "Here, have a bunch of kids!" At first glance, some people might wonder if that was a blessing or a curse!

But a deeper look into the heart of God, as re-vealed from cover to cover in the Bible, shows that children are regarded as *blessings* from Him. When God wanted to bless someone in the Bible, that blessing often took the form of a child.

When God "blessed" Adam and Eve, telling them to be fruitful and multiply, they did—having one child, then two, then three, and then *"other sons and daughters" (see Genesis 5:4).*

When God "blessed" Abraham and Sarah, He gave them a child, and told them that their de-scendants would one day be *"as numerous as the stars of the sky and as the sand on the seashore" (see Genesis 22:17-18).*

When God "blessed" Job after all of the tragedy that Job went through, God gave him all kinds of "stuff"—and ten children! Those chil-dren had children of their own, who had children of their own, who had children of their own. Job was eventually able to see *"his children and their chil-dren to the fourth generation" (see Job 42:12-16).*

I've noticed that most self-help books that talk about how to have a more blessed sex life rarely, if ever, mention the blessings of children that result from sex. But from God's point of view, the blessing of sex and the blessing of children go together, which brings us back full circle to the twin purposes for which God created sex in the first place: for intimacy and fruitfulness.

This is not to say that if we don't have children, or if we have only one child or a few children that we are not blessed by God. As I've read through the Bible, God doesn't give an optimal number of children for anyone. Sarah had one, Rebekah had two, Eve had many—Jesus didn't have any. What I do find in the Bible is that each of these people viewed children as blessings from God regardless of how many, if any, they had.

But getting God's mindset about children doesn't always come naturally.

GETTING GOD'S MINDSET

When I was about twelve, an exchange student from another country lived with our family. When she told us about her family and how she and her ten brothers and sisters all lived in a small house in what we would consider poverty, we felt sorry for her. There were three of us kids in our family and we felt rich by comparison. What a shock it was to later hear that her father felt sorry for us! *How poor that family must be,* he thought, *to have so few children.*

I had to rethink my definition of what it means to be rich and what it means to be poor! Several years later, when I was about to marry Lana, I had to rethink my definition even more!

As Lana and I talked about our future together, she told me that she wanted to have twelve kids! She came from a family of nine and said that she always wished there were more kids around to play with. In my family of three kids, I was thrilled whenever I had the peace and quiet of the house all to myself. Somebody's mindset was going to have to change!

With our wedding just a few months away, I began to pray that God would give us the exact number of children *He* wanted us to have. Six kids later, I'm still praying!

As I began to read the Bible on the subject of

children, I began to see that person after person viewed children as blessings.

When King Solomon wrote about children, he said, *"Blessed is the man whose quiver is full of them"* *(Psalm 127:5a)*. When Mary found out she was pregnant with Jesus, she said, *"From now on all generations will call me blessed..." (Luke 1:48b)*. When some little children came up to Jesus, the disciples tried to "shoo" them away. Jesus responded with these classic words, *"Let the little children come to me, and do not hinder them, for the kingdom of heaven belongs to such as these" (Matthew 19:14)*. Whether we have one child, ten children or no children, God wants our *hearts* towards children to be the same as His: viewing them as blessings *from* Him and blessings *to* Him.

While my mindset towards children began to change when I got married, to be honest, my heart didn't catch up until Lana was pregnant with our third child. Not that I wasn't thrilled for the first two! But with the uncertainty of what to expect during the first pregnancy and with the health complications that Lana experienced early on with the second, it wasn't until the third preg-

nancy that I was finally able to relax and genuinely *feel* that God was blessing me. In fact, I felt it
so strongly when I found out Lana was pregnant
for the third time, we decided to name our third
child with *two* names that mean "blessing"—a
double blessing! I felt that I could finally see the
true blessing of children from God's point of
view.

Sex, with God's Blessing

As our view of sex lines up more and more
with God's view of sex, the blessings that come
from sex become much more evident. Bill Alli-
son, the founder of Cadre Ministries, tells the story about a time when he was praying the prayer
of Jabez and asking God to expand his borders.
When his wife became pregnant with their sixth
child, she said, "He prayed, and I'm the one who
got expanded!"

Having God's mindset about children can
change the actual experience of sex, too. To
make love with your spouse without fear of pregnancy, but actually thinking about it and looking

forward to it as a blessing from God, is enough to knock your socks off. Sex can be more fun and more exciting when there's no holding back, knowing that what you're doing is with the full knowledge of, consent of, and *blessing of* God.

For me, when Lana's been pregnant, our times of intimacy have been just as enjoyable, if not more so. Perhaps it has something to do with knowing that the child conceived within her has been conceived as a result of our lovemaking, not to mention the fact that her hormones double daily during pregnancy.

On the other hand, someone might rightfully ask: "But isn't it a lot of work to take care of kids?" Absolutely!

As blessings of *any kind* increase, so do the responsibilities. Jesus says:

"From everyone who has been given much, much will be demanded; and from the one who has been entrusted with much, much more will be asked" (Luke 12:48b).

Anyone who actually owns two or three vacation homes or two or three cars—let alone nine or ten—would attest to this fact. Between all of the maintenance, repairs, taxes, insurance, and the ongoing investment of time, all these things can threaten to steal the joy from even the most enthusiastic homeowner or car lover. The key to keeping your joy is keeping God's perspective at the forefront of your mind—not a trivial task some days!—but a task that can turn something that might feel like a burden back into the blessing that God intended it to be.

God wants us to get His perspective on life, which doesn't always come naturally. As God says:

"For my thoughts are not your thoughts, neither are your ways my ways," declares the Lord. "As the heavens are higher than the earth so are my ways higher than your ways and my thoughts than your thoughts" (Isaiah 55:8-9).

But when we ask Him to, God will help us to close the gap between His thoughts and ways and ours. And when He does, it can make all the difference in the world, as I'll share in the next and final chapter.

REVIEW QUESTIONS

1. *When God blessed Adam and Eve, with what did He bless them? (Genesis 1:28, Genesis 5:4)*
2. *What are some other examples from the Bible where children were viewed as blessings? (Genesis 22:17-18, Job 42:12-16, Psalm 127:5, Luke 1:48)*
3. *What also increases as the blessings of God increase? (Luke 12:48)*
4. *How different are our thoughts and ways compared to God's? (Isaiah 55:8-9)*

7

The Difference God Makes

*"Therefore everyone who hears these words of mine
and puts them into practice is like a wise man
who built his house on the rock."*
Matthew 7:24

There's so much more I still want to tell you. There's so much more *God* still wants to tell you! But I hope that what I've told you so far will give you a good foundation for everything else that God says about sex.

While there are many other issues that I could address here, and that God does address in the Bible, I feel that those I've covered so far will help to put many of the others into place.

The evangelist D. L. Moody said, "The best way to show that a stick is crooked is not to argue about it or to spend time denouncing it, but to lay a straight stick alongside it."[1] I hope this book will serve as a "straight stick" for you as you come across other issues related to sex.

Here's a recap of some of the main points I hope you've gotten from this book so far:

1) *God created sex for the twin purposes of intimacy and fruitfulness.* God loves people and He doesn't want them to be alone. Through sex, He's made a way to fulfill the desires of His heart, while at the same time fulfilling the desires of our hearts.

2) *God wants us to stay pure both before and within marriage.* God wants us to treat others as if they're someone else's husband or wife until the day that we marry them, because until that day, they still might be.

3) *God wants us to flee from temptation.* God knows what it's like to be tempted and He will always provide us a way out of temptation if we'll look for it and take it. God wants us to learn to control our bodies, to

pray against temptation, and to *run* from it!

4) *God wants us to confess our sins so we can become pure again.* God doesn't want Satan to keep us down when we sin. By confessing our sins to Him and putting our faith in Jesus, God promises to forgive us of our sins so that we can live the life He's called us to live, both here on earth and on into heaven.

5) *God wants us to know our spouse intimately and regularly.* God wants us to take time to know the husband or wife He has created for us, both before *and* after marriage. The better we know them, the better we can treat them as the gifts from God that they truly are.

6) *God wants us to view children as blessings.* By asking God to give us His mindset towards children, we can't help but experience His blessings, regardless of how many, if any, children God might give us.

Before I close, I'd like to share with you the

most profound difference that God has made in my life when I finally put into practice what He says about sex. There's no doubt that God wants us to *know* what He says about sex. But knowing what He says and putting it into practice are two different things. Jesus said it this way:

"Therefore everyone who hears these words of mine and puts them into practice is like a wise man who built his house on the rock. The rain came down, the streams rose, and the winds blew and beat against that house; yet it did not fall, because it had its foundation on the rock. But everyone who hears these words of mine and does not put them into practice is like a foolish man who built his house on sand. The rain came down, the streams rose, and the winds blew and beat against that house, and it fell with a great crash" (Matthew 7:24-27).

Have you heard the story about the five frogs who were sitting on a log when one of them decided to jump off? How many frogs were still left on the log? All five! One of them had only *decided* to jump off.

It's one thing to *decide* to do what God says; it's another to take the leap of faith and actually *do* it. But when you do, hang on! God will do for you more than all you could ask or imagine.

I know, because I've taken that leap myself.

THE DIFFERENCE GOD HAS MADE FOR ME

I mentioned in the dedication of this book that my children might not be here today if it weren't for the things I learned from God and have shared in this book. I wasn't kidding!

When I was living for my own desires, doing whatever *felt* good, I was on a path headed towards destruction and didn't even know it. I was just following my desires wherever they led me.

For a few years in college, my desires even led me into homosexuality, being sexually intimate with other men. These relationships seemed to fulfill a valid need I had for close friendships with other men. I didn't realize that the way I was fulfilling that need wasn't the way God wanted me to fulfill it. I was just having fun, not realizing the danger that this presented to my life, nor the danger that this presented to God's plan for my future.

The term *AIDS* was a new word at that time to describe the deadly condition that many homosexual men were contracting from their sexual activity with one another. It never occurred to me that I could possibly get AIDS until several years later, just a few days after I had put my faith in Christ. But that same week, someone happened to ask me if I had ever been tested for AIDS. I hadn't, so I went in for a test. That's when it hit me: what I had been doing wasn't just about fun and games, it was about life and death. In the following week, as I waited for the results of the test to come back, I was afraid for my life. I wasn't afraid for my soul, because I had already put my faith in Christ. I knew that God had forgiven me and that He would bring me to live with Him in heaven, even if I did die. But I didn't want to die. I wanted to live the fullest possible life that God had created me to live.

You can imagine my relief when they gave me the results: I *didn't* have AIDS. I don't know why I was spared when others haven't been, whether they're Christians or not. It certainly wasn't because I deserved it. But I knew that whatever the reason, I now had another shot at life. I felt as if God had picked me up off the path of death and had put me on the path of life, and life abundant.

On this new path, God has given me a wife and six kids as a result of our sexual intimacy— life *abundant!*

What difference can it make to follow God's plan for your life instead of your own? For me, for my wife, and for our six kids who might never have been born, it's made all the difference in the world.

GOD'S BLESSING FOR YOU

The evangelist Billy Graham once gave a clear and concise summary of the difference God makes in our sex lives:

"Sex is the most wonderful thing on this earth, as long as God is in it. When the Devil gets in it, it's the most terrible thing on earth."[2]

I couldn't agree more. If for any reason sex ever becomes, or has already become, one of the most terrible things on earth for you, I want to encourage you to keep turning to God and keep putting your faith in Him for everything in your life. Ask Him to give you a new vision for how He wants you to view and experience sex. There's too much at stake for you to wait any longer—for you, for those around you, and for those who may not yet even be born.

Ask God to pick you up and put you on His path of life *abundant,* to send His Holy Spirit to keep you on that path, and to bless your life beyond all you could ask or imagine.

When you do, you'll find that God is faithful. When you delight yourself in Him, He *will* give you the desires of your heart. That's a promise straight from the Word of God:

"Delight yourself in the LORD and he will give you the desires of your heart" (Psalm 37:4).

And it's my heartfelt prayer for you.

*"May He give you the desire of your heart
and make all your plans succeed.
We will shout for joy when you are victorious
and will lift up our banners in the name of our God.
May the Lord grant all your requests."
Psalm 20:4-5*

REVIEW QUESTIONS

1. *How would you summarize at least three things that God says about sex in the Bible?*
2. *What did Jesus say the difference would be between those who hear what God says and those who do what God says? (Matthew 7:24-27)*
3. *What difference did it make in the life of the author to get God's perspective on sex?*
4. *What does God promise to give you if you delight yourself in Him? (Psalm 37:4)*

Endnotes:

[1] *Love is the Greatest*, George Sweeting, p. 81
[2] *Just As I Am*, Billy Graham, p. 244

Appendix

WHAT IS SEX, ANYWAY?

"For this reason a man will leave his father and mother and be united to his wife, and they will become one flesh."
Genesis 2:24

S
ex is the process by which many living things reproduce, from plants, trees and animals, to birds, fish and people.

Sex is also one of the most incredible processes ever conceived in the mind of God. I've been at the birth of each of my children, and the way a child is born is astounding. But I've also been at the *conception* of each of my children, that moment in time when they were created, and I can say that the way a child is conceived in the first place is equally astounding, if not more so!

I'd like to describe that process to you here, as God has revealed it to us through the design of nature itself. Although I've taken great care to describe this process in a simple way, don't mistake my simple description for a simple process. The human reproductive system is one of the most intricate and complex systems ever created.

Sex 101

Babies are very fragile and need a safe place to grow, so God created just such a place inside each woman called a *womb*. The womb is made of a soft, expandable tissue that gently cuddles a baby.

But a baby doesn't start as a full-grown baby; it starts as a tiny egg, smaller than the dot at the end of this sentence. When a woman reaches *puberty*, the age when she's old enough to start having children, God designed her body to begin to release eggs into her womb. About once every month, an egg is released from a small holding area, called an *ovary*, just above the womb. When the ovary releases the egg, the egg glides down a thin tube towards the womb. There are two of these ovaries and two of these tubes that lead into the womb. The ovaries take turns every other month releasing eggs.

The egg gradually makes its way towards the womb waiting to be *fertilized*, something I'll discuss below. If the egg isn't fertilized within a few days, it simply travels on through the womb and down a larger tube that comes out of a woman's body called the *vagina*. The vagina is the central opening of the three openings between a woman's legs. The *urethra*, where the urine, or liquid waste comes out, is in front of the vagina, and the *rectum*, where the bowel movements, or solid waste comes out, is behind it.

The egg that comes out of the vagina is too small to be seen, but some of the blood that lines the inside walls of the womb does come out with the egg as a way of cleansing the womb before the process starts all over again. Because this flow of blood containing the egg usually happens about once a month, or periodically, people call this monthly flow a *period*.

The next month, the process starts over and another egg is released from the other ovary. This egg then travels down the tube, called the *fallopian tube*, towards the womb, also called the *uterus*, to be possibly fertilized. If the egg isn't fertilized, it travels on through the womb and down the vagina, then comes out with the blood from the womb in the next period.

The release of eggs within a woman is important, but without fertilization, a baby can't be created. Fertilization is the spark that creates a new life. Fertilization occurs when something called a *sperm* comes into contact with an egg. Sperm are also very tiny; they're even smaller than the egg.

But a woman's body doesn't produce sperm. Sperm are only produced inside a man's body. Just as a woman's body contains two ovaries where eggs are stored, a man's body contains two *testicles* where sperm are produced. These two testicles are held in a sack of skin, called the *scrotum,* found between a man's legs. The sperm must be kept a little cooler than the rest of the body, so God created this sack to hang just outside the man's body to keep the temperature just right.

When a man gets old enough to start having children, his testicles begin to produce sperm. Since a sperm and an egg must come into contact with each other in order to create a child, God designed a way to get the sperm and egg together without ever having to travel outside a human body. And the way God brings the sperm and egg together is through this incredible experience called *sex*.

Our bodies are wired with special nerves near the surface of our skin that can make us feel great when someone gives us a hug or a kiss. But God has saved a romantic kind of hugging and kissing that we can enjoy with our husbands or wives that can feel even more amazing.

During these special times of hugging and kissing, a man's penis is stimulated by all the touching so that it becomes straight and firm, even though it's still soft to the touch. The penis becomes this way as blood rushes into it and flows into a unique type of body tissue found only in the penis.

As the man and woman snuggle closer to each other, his penis begins to release a smooth, clear, lotion-like fluid called *semen*. In the same way, the woman's body releases a similarly smooth and clear fluid that lubricates her vagina, the tube that leads into her womb. All of this naturally produced lotion makes the rubbing and touching even more smooth and wonderful.

God has designed the woman's vagina to be soft and expandable so that her husband's penis can fit softly and snugly inside it. As a man and woman continue to love each other in this way, with his penis gently rubbing inside her vagina, the rubbing movements eventually trigger millions of these minuscule sperm to be released from the testicles and they combine with the semen, giving the semen a milky-white appearance. The combined sperm and semen then travel up through the penis and into the woman's vagina and then on into the woman's womb.

The release of sperm from the man's body is called an *ejaculation*. At this climactic moment, both the man and woman will often feel an intensely pleasurable sensation called an *orgasm*. In this way, God is able to get the sperm from the man's body into the womb of the woman's body without ever having to travel outside the human body!

If one of the woman's ovaries has already released an egg into the tube leading to the womb, the first sperm to reach the egg and come into contact with it sparks the process of fertilization. When that happens, a moment called *conception,* a new life is created and begins to grow in the womb.

After the sperm has been released from the man into the woman, the man's penis begins to relax, and the husband and wife can continue to hold each other, hugging and kissing as long as they want.

The biological term for this process is *sexual intercourse,* which is usually just shortened to the word *sex.* Because this process feels so great and makes a husband and wife feel so loved by each other, the experience is sometimes called *making love.*

God calls it becoming *one flesh:*

"For this reason a man will leave his father and mother and be united to his wife, and they will become one flesh" (Genesis 2:24).

I call it a miracle! I've never experienced any-thing like it in all my life.

When I first learned about sex, I thought that it was one of the most unusual things I had ever heard. But since then, I've learned that it's not unusual at all to God. This is the process He's been using for thousands of years to create new life.

If you ever have questions about sex, or about *anything* for that matter, ask God to give you His wisdom. He'll be glad to pour it out on you in abundance:

"If any of you lacks wisdom, he should ask God, who gives generously to all without finding fault, and it will be given to him" (James 1:5).

REVIEW QUESTIONS

1. *What two things does God bring together through sex to create a child—one from a woman's body and one from a man's?*
2. *What happens to a woman's egg if it has not been fertilized within a certain period of time?*
3. *What does God say that a man and his wife become when they are united together? (Genesis 2:24)*

4. *What does God promise to give generously to those who ask Him for it? (James 1:5)*

About the Author

Described by *USA Today* as "a new breed of evangelist," Eric Elder is an ordained pastor, the father of six kids, and the creator of *The Ranch,* a faith-boosting website that attracts thousands of visitors each month at THERANCH.ORG.

Eric is also an inspirational writer and speaker, having written about God for publications like Billy Graham's *Decision Magazine,* and spoken about sex at national conferences like the *Exodus International Freedom Conference.*

By combining the topics of God and sex into this one book, Eric has created a short work that speaks volumes. Adults will appreciate his helpful insights and practical wisdom, parents will appreciate his tasteful approach to a delicate subject, and teens and pre-teens will appreciate his openness, honesty, and sense of humor which are woven throughout the pages of this book.

To listen to, download, or order more resources from the *What God Says™* series, visit:

WHATGODSAYS.COM